Rick Hansen

Improving Life for People with Disabilities

Adrianna Morganelli

Crabtree Publishing Company
www.crabtreebooks.com

Author: Adrianna Morganelli

Series research and development: Reagan Miller

Editorial director: Kathy Middleton

Editor: Crystal Sikkens

Proofreader: Janine Deschenes

Photo researcher: Crystal Sikkens

Designer and prepress technician: Samara Parent

Print coordinator: Katherine Berti

Photographs:
AP Images: ©AP Photo: page 10; ©Neal Ulevich: page 18; ©Inoue: page 19

The Canadian Press: ©COC/J Merrithew: page 11; ©Jon Murray: page 21; ©Patrick Doyle: page 22; ©Jonathan Hayward: page 25; ©Chuck Stoody: page 26; ©Globe and Mail/The Canadian Press/John Lehmann: page 27; ©Chris Young: pages 28-29

Getty Images: ©Jim Ross: title page; ©Mike Slaughter: pages 4-5; ©Boris Spremo: pages 12-13, 20

iStock: ©Ann Steer: pages 16-17

Keystone: ©Paulinus Hardi Subiantoro: page 15

Superstock: ©Stan Navratil: pages 6-7

University of British Columbia: ©University of British Columbia Archives, Photo by Martin Dee [UBC 44.1/577-3]: page 8; ©University of British Columbia Archives [UBC 35.2/78-2]: page 9

Wikimedia Commons: ©Andybremner2012: page 6 (inset); ©KyleAndMelissa22: page 14; ©Urban Mixer (Raj Taneja): cover, page 30

All other images from Shutterstock

Library and Archives Canada Cataloguing in Publication

Morganelli, Adrianna, 1979-, author
    Rick Hansen : improving life for people with disabilities
/ Adrianna Morganelli.

(Remarkable lives revealed)
Includes index.
Issued in print and electronic formats.
ISBN 978-0-7787-2692-0 (hardback).--
ISBN 978-0-7787-2703-3--(paperback).--ISBN 978-1-4271-1813-4 (html)

    1. Hansen, Rick, 1957- --Juvenile literature. 2. Human rights
workers--Canada--Biography--Juvenile literature. 3. Paraplegics--
Canada--Biography--Juvenile literature. 4. Olympic athletes--
Canada--Biography--Juvenile literature. 5. Athletes with
disabilities--Canada--Biography--Juvenile literature. I. Title.

RD796.H35M67 2016   j362.4'3092   C2016-904113-1
                                              C2016-904114-X

Library of Congress Cataloging-in-Publication Data

Names: Morganelli, Adrianna, 1979- author.
Title: Rick Hansen : improving life for people with disabilities /
    Adrianna Morganelli.
Description: New York : Crabtree Publishing Company, [2017] |
    Series: Remarkable lives revealed | Includes index. |
    Audience: Ages: 7-10. | Audience: Grades: 4 to 6.
Identifiers: LCCN 2016026659 |
    ISBN 9780778726920 (Reinforced library binding) |
    ISBN 9780778727033 (Paperback) |
    ISBN 9781427118134 (Electronic HTML)
Subjects: LCSH: Hansen, Rick, 1957- | Human rights
    workers--Canada--Biography--Juvenile literature. | Athletes with
    disabilities--Canada--Biography--Juvenile literature. |
    Paraplegics--Canada--Biography--Juvenile literature.
Classification: LCC RC406.P3 M67 2017 | DDC 796.04/56092 [B] --de
LC record available at https://lccn.loc.gov/2016026659

Crabtree Publishing Company
www.crabtreebooks.com   1-800-387-7650

Printed in Canada/082016/TL20160715

**Published
in Canada**
Crabtree Publishing
616 Welland Ave.
St. Catharines, Ontario
L2M 5V6

**Published in
the United States**
Crabtree Publishing
PMB 59051
350 Fifth Ave., 59th Floor
New York, NY 10118

**Published in the
United Kingdom**
Crabtree Publishing
Maritime House
Basin Road North, Hove
BN41 1WR

**Published
in Australia**
Crabtree Publishing
3 Charles Street
Coburg North
VIC, 3058

Contents

On the Move

Everyone has their own idea of what makes a person remarkable. A remarkable person may have qualities you admire. They may be someone that inspires you or that you look up to. A person's story can be shared through a biography. We can learn a lot from the biographies of others. As you read about the story of Rick Hansen, think about the qualities he has that have helped make his achievements possible, and why so many people describe him as remarkable.

> *I try to encourage people to never give up on their dreams and to look at what you can do - not what you can't do.*
>
> **—Rick Hansen,**
> **www.rickhansen.com**

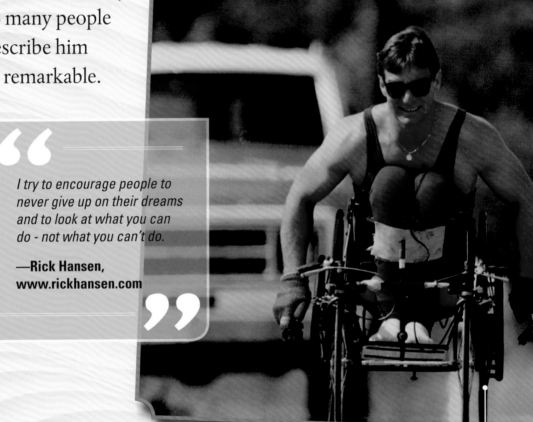

Rick persevered through pain and harsh environments on his tour around the world to bring awareness to the limitless abilities of people who have disabilities.

an in Motion"

ter becoming a **paraplegic** due to an accident, Rick Hansen
dicated his life to proving the potential of people with disabilities.
is best known as the "Man in Motion" for his famous two-year
eelchair trip around the world. Wheeling close to 25,000 miles
,000 kilometers) through 34 countries, Rick raised millions of
llars for research to find a cure for paralysis from **spinal cord**
ury. His perseverance and determination inspired countless people
th disabilities to accomplish their dreams.

? THINK ABOUT IT

Is there someone in your life
that you find remarkable?
What qualities do they have
that you find remarkable?

What is a Biography?

A biography is a description of a person's life. Biographies
help us understand how others experienced events, and
how their lives have influenced and affected other people.
Biographies can be based on many sources of information.
Primary sources include a person's own words or pictures.
Secondary sources include stories from friends, family,
media, and research.

Early Childhood

Rick Hansen was born in Port Alberni, British Columbia, Canada, on August 26, 1957, to Joan and Marvin Hansen. He and his three younger siblings, Brad, Cindy, and Christine, grew up in Williams Lake, British Columbia. As a child, Rick was a natural athlete, and enjoyed playing basketball, volleyball, and rugby. He had always dreamed of one day participating in the Olympic Games. He loved the outdoors, and spent a lot of time fishing with family and friends.

agedy Strikes

hile in high school, Rick was in an accident that would change his e forever. On June 27, 1973, he and his friend Don Adler were riding the back of a pickup truck on their way home from a week-long hing trip. As the truck drove along a steep, winding road, it went t of control and crashed. Don and Rick were thrown from the ick. The crash left Rick with a broken back and severed spinal cord. couldn't feel or move his legs. The doctors told Rick that he was w paralyzed from the waist down, and that he would never walk in. He was just 15 years old.

A Sudden Blow

Rick was devastated by his sudden fate to live the rest of his life as a paraplegic. He had to now use a wheelchair to get around, which made him feel that he wasn't the same person that he was before his injury. He was afraid that people would now treat him differently, and he didn't want to feel dependent on others.

Williams Lake is a city located in the interior of British Columbia. The city itself has a population of just over 11,000 people.

A New Life

Rick underwent seven months of **rehabilitation** in Vancouver. When he returned home, he had to learn to adapt to his new life in a wheelchair. With the support of his family and friends, Rick began to realize that he was able to do a lot of the things he once did before his accident, such as fishing and playing sports. Rick began to play wheelchair sports, including basketball, volleyball, and tennis. With inspiration from his high school coach, Bob Redford, he excelled.

Attitude adjustment

Adjusting to his new life was not easy, but Rick soon realized that although he had to face many new challenges, his biggest challenge was changing his own attitude toward his disability.

? THINK ABOUT IT

Imagine having the life you are used to being suddenly changed forever. What parts of your life would you never want changed?

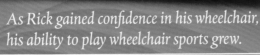

As Rick gained confidence in his wheelchair, his ability to play wheelchair sports grew.

Career in Sports

ob Redford also encouraged Rick to pursue his dream of ecoming a physical education teacher. He applied to the niversity of British Columbia, ut his application got rejected. ather than accept defeat, Rick onvinced the faculty to give him chance. He enrolled in 1976, nd became the first person with physical disability to graduate om the university with a degree a Physical Education!

> "
> —————
>
> *When I was young, people took the time to explain the importance of personal achievement and determination to me. I was continually challenged and inspired to make my life all that it could be, to constantly focus on the things I can do.*
>
> **—Rick Hansen,**
> **www.rickhansen.com**
>
> ,,

Rick received an honorary degree at the University of British Columbia in 1987.

Once an Athlete, Always an Athlete

After his accident, Rick set new goals for his life. While at the University of British Columbia, he was recruited by coach Stan Stronge to join the Vancouver Cablecars wheelchair basketball team. Between 1976 and 1982, Rick led his team to win six national championships. In 1979, he became dedicated to wheelchair racing, and began traveling around the world competing in wheelchair marathons, winning 19 international races.

Rick Hansen broke his own record at the Honolulu Wheelchair Marathon with a time of two hours, three minutes, and 21 seconds.

lympic dreams

ck's early dream of competing in e Olympic Games did not leave him ter his injury. Rick competed in the ralympic Summer Games in 1980 d 1984, winning six medals. In 1982, won nine gold medals in the Pan nerican Games. Finally, in 1984, Rick's lympic dream was finally achieved when competed at the Olympic Games in heelchair track as an **exhibition sport**. presenting Canada in the race, he was e first person to break the two-hour cord in a wheelchair marathon!

Carrying the Flame

When the Winter Olympics came to Vancouver, British Columbia (B.C.) in 2010, the Olympic torch was carried across Canada in a relay. Rick was chosen to carry the torch from his home in Richmond, B.C., to Vancouver.

Rick Hansen and Canadian teammate Mel Fitzgerald (left) compete at the 1984 Summer Olympic Games in Los Angeles.

A Man in Motion

With Rick's success in wheelchair sports came renewed courage and determination. After his friend Terry Fox embarked on his Marathon of Hope in 1980 to raise money for cancer research, Rick was inspired to make a difference in the lives of people who have disabilities. He decided to circle the world in his wheelchair to help find a cure for spinal injuries, and to help shape a more **inclusive** world for people with disabilities by proving that they still have many physical abilities.

> " I had an amazing team. They challenged, encouraged and supported me and asked nothing in return. I feel incredibly privileged to have had them with me. Without them, the dream would have been absolutely impossible.
>
> —Rick Hansen,
> www.rickhansen.com "

e Wheels Start Turning

owing that he couldn't accomplish his goal alone, Rick gathered
o teams made up of people who shared his commitment to his
eam. The team that remained at home base in Vancouver would
lp plan Rick's route and collect donations. The road crew, which
cluded Don Alder and Rick's **physiotherapist** Amanda Reid, would
vel with him around the world, following on foot, by bike, and in
e motor home they would share. Rick named his mission the Man
Motion World Tour.

Love on the Road

Rick Hansen and his physiotherapist Amanda Reid fell in love during the Man in Motion World Tour. They became engaged during the tour's second year, and today they are married and have three daughters, Emma, Alana, and Rebecca.

Rick Hansen's team not only gave him emotional support on the tour, but also trekked beside him on his journey around the world.

And He's Off!

On March 21, 1985, Rick waved goodbye to the crowd gathered at Oakridge Mall, in Vancouver, before setting off on his tour. Over the next three weeks, Rick wheeled into the United States, through Washington, Oregon, California, and across San Francisco's Golden Gate Bridge. By this time, Rick and his team were disappointed in the amount of public attention and support they were receiving, but the school children and honking drivers they encountered along the roads helped motivate them to continue.

At the beginning of Rick's tour, he wheeled 2,000 feet (610 meters) up the summit of the Siskiyou Mountains in Oregon.

David Foster co-wrote and played the keyboard in the song "St. Elmo's Fire."

Spark of Interest

terest in Rick's tour began to grow when Canadian Grammy award-
nning musician and composer David Foster co-wrote the song
t. Elmo's Fire" in his honor. As the song topped charts around
e world, awareness of the Man in Motion World Tour grew. Day
ter day, Rick and his team continued to fight for their cause. After
heeling through Los Angeles and San Diego, Rick pushed himself
rough the sweltering heat of the desert states of Arizona, New
exico, Texas, Louisiana, Mississippi, and Alabama. On June 24,
ck made it to Miami, Florida, raising about $6,000 in donations and
aveling about 4,700 miles (7,563 kilometers) from home!

Wheeling Through Europe

In the summer of 1985, Rick began the European part of the tour, where he and his team were met with warmth and generosity. When in London, England, the Queen's motorcycle **escort** blocked traffic so that Rick could wheel across the London Bridge. They boarded a ferry to France, and traveled throughout Belgium, Netherlands, and West Germany. The team was greeted by well-wishers throughout Denmark, Sweden, and Norway, and they reached the 7,000-mile (11,265-kilometer) mark while in Finland, where Rick celebrated his 28th birthday.

I was continually challenged and inspired to make my life all that it could be, to constantly focus on the things I can do. The Man in Motion World Tour was my journey around the world to make a difference.

—Rick Hansen, www.rickhansen.com

ck wheeled through Poland, the Austrian Alps, Switzerland, ance, Spain, and Portugal before entering Italy, where Pope John ul II blessed the remainder of the tour. When Rick and his team ached Greece, they celebrated with glasses of champagne to lebrate reaching the final portion of their European tour. Rick then heeled 30 miles (48 kilometers) on the island of Bahrain before ing to Jordan, where he wheeled over the Allenby Bridge, linking rdan and Israel. Their trip to the Middle East ended in Tel Aviv, here the team prepared for its long flight to New Zealand.

Hardships

Every day Rick woke at dawn to wheel about 72 miles (115 kilometers), the equivalent of two marathons, despite injuries to his shoulders, wrists and hands, and fatigue. Wheeling about eight hours every day, Rick persevered through windstorms and torrential rain, snow, and ice. He wheeled over rough terrain, mountains, oceans, and deserts. Even when on flat roadways, Rick had to watch out for drivers. Whenever Rick felt like giving up, his team and supporters encouraged him to continue wheeling through one country after another.

England's historic London Bridge spans across the Thames River.

A Long Way Home

By 1986, Rick Hansen and his team had completed the first year of their tour. After 12,450 miles (20,036 kilometers), the team arrived in Australia, which was the halfway point. By this time, their confidence had grown. They knew that if they could make it halfway around the world, they could complete the rest of the distance. In the spring, Rick arrived in China. While in Beijing, Rick's goal was to wheel up the Great Wall of China.

Ups and Downs

Upon reaching the halfway mark, Rick's motor home had been robbed four times. The new year began with more than $3,000 of equipment, including extra wheelchairs, being stolen. Rick had worn out 47 pairs of gloves while making 7,180,800 wheelchair strokes, and his wheelchairs had had 63 flat tires!

Even though it was extremely difficult to climb the 60-degree inclines of the Great Wall of China, Rick summoned his strength and slowly wheeled his way to the top. Supporters, media, and tourists were right behind him, cheering him on.

Wheeling through Asia

As he wheeled on to Shanghai, China, thousands of people threw flowers in his path and celebrated his achievements. Rick had won the hearts of the people, and gathered the largest crowds of the tour. Rick completed the Asian part of the tour wheeling through South Korea and Japan, where they met the emperor.

While in Japan, Rick and his team were greeted by Princess Michiko and Crown Prince Akihito.

On His Way Home

While traveling in the United States on his journey back to Canada, Rick was inspired to find that the media and public were well aware of the Man in Motion World Tour. His fellow Canadians were excited for their hero's return home, and support for Rick's cause grew. As Rick wheeled along the roads of Newfoundland, people ran to donate money, totaling more than $97,000. He wheeled from Quebec into Ottawa, Ontario, where he received a $1 million cheque from the government.

Prime Minister Brian Mulroney delivered a cheque for $1 million to Rick on Parliament Hill, in Ottawa.

Hero's Welcome!

On May 22, 1987, Rick and the team wheeled across the Port Mann Bridge into Vancouver. Thousands of cheering people lined the streets to the Oakridge Mall, where they had begun their journey two years, two months, and two days before. Rick crossed the finish line, and the Man in Motion World Tour was finally over. He had wheeled 24,900 miles (40,072 kilometers). Wheeling through 34 countries and four continents, Rick and his team raised a whopping 26 million for spinal cord research, rehabilitation, and wheelchair sports. Most importantly, Rick had succeeded in helping lessen the negative stigmas attributed to people with disabilities.

In Vancouver, Rick Hansen wheeled through the yellow ribbon marking the end of his Man in Motion World Tour.

? THINK ABOUT IT

Who are the people in your life that you would want to accompany you on an important journey?

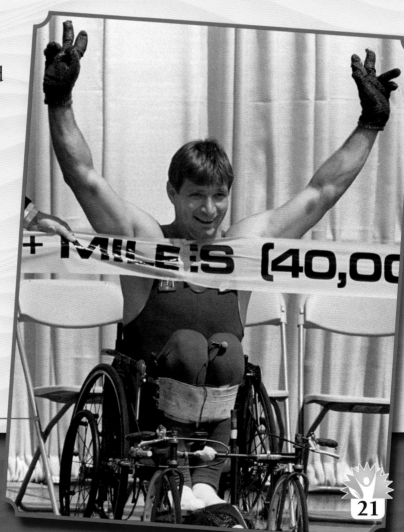

Just the Beginning

Rick Hansen became an international hero after the Man in Motion World Tour, but he felt that his activism was only just beginning. Mo work needed to be done to make public places more accessible to all people, regardless of their physical abilities. In 1988, Rick founded t Rick Hansen Foundation, which has raised more than $250 million research and programs related to spinal cord injuries.

In 2007, the Canadian government granted $30 million to the Spinal Cord Injury Transnational Research Network. Rick Hansen was awarded the funding by former Prime Minister Stephen Harper in Ottawa.

chool Program

...ck's foundation is made up of several programs that aim to create ...inclusive world. Thousands of schools across Canada have adopted ...he Rick Hansen School Program, which educates children about ...ysical disabilities and the barriers that people who have disabilities ...ce every day. The program aims to reduce bullying and empower ...ung people to make a difference.

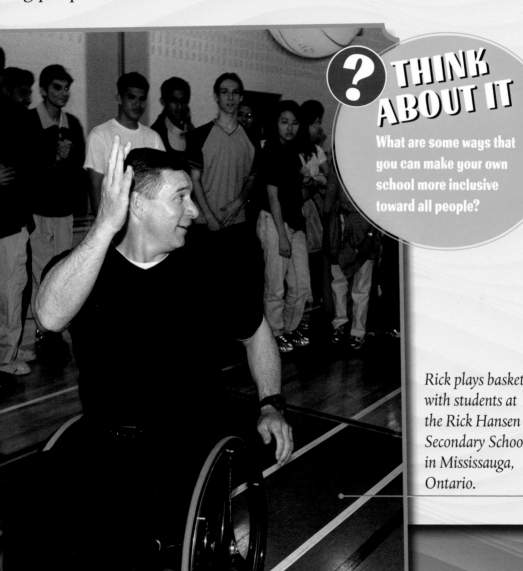

? THINK ABOUT IT

What are some ways that you can make your own school more inclusive toward all people?

Rick plays basketball with students at the Rick Hansen Secondary School in Mississauga, Ontario.

National Access Awareness Week

Rick Hansen's foundation worked with the Canadian government to create National Access Awareness Week, which is held in the spring each year. Thousands of communities across Canada participate in events such as scavenger hunts and public BBQs, and focus on improving access to public places such as parks and community centers so that people with disabilities can become more involved in their communities.

NATIONAL ACCESS WEEK

MAY 29 - JUNE 4, 2016

ck believes that teamwork is key to success, and dreamed of a ace where doctors could work together to find a cure for paralysis e to spinal cord injuries. In 2008, he established the Rick Hansen stitute, located in the Blusson Spinal Cord Centre, in Vancouver. ere, countless experts work as eam to find ways to prevent inal injuries, care for people th paralysis, and find a cure that paralyzed people may meday be able to walk again.

> " I believe that one day the wheelchair will be something you'll see in a museum.
>
> —Rick Hansen, www.rickhansen.com "

The Countess of Wessex, England, Sophie Rhys-Jones, visited the Blusson Spinal Cord Centre, where a patient demonstrated how a new walking device works.

Hansen's Other Passions

Ever since he was a child, Rick has had a passion to play sports. He still loves to play wheelchair basketball and volleyball, but he also enjoys tennis, skiing, kayaking, and **pilates**. He believes that playing sports helps to unite people, and inspires young people to achieve their goals. Today, Rick still supports wheelchair sports, and volunteers his time coaching athletes.

Celebrating 25 Years!

In 2011, the Rick Hansen Foundation established the Rick Hansen 25th Anniversary Relay to commemorate the anniversary of Rick's Man in Motion World Tour. More than 7,000 people took place in the relay race, which covered 7,457 miles (12,000 kilometers), and retraced the original route that Rick wheeled across Canada. The relay began in Newfoundland, and it took nine months for the participants to run, walk, and wheel westward to British Columbia.

Rick enjoys visiting schools and community centers to speak with other wheelchair athletes.

...hing is one of Rick's favorite things to do. Here, he ...es in the Fraser River in British Columbia.

...sh Conservation

...ick learned to fish when he was just three years old, and fishing ...s become his favorite pastime ever since. His love of fishing and ...terest in environmental issues prompted him to establish the ...cific Salmon Endowment Fund Society in 2000. The organization ...elps to protect the salmon population of the waters in British ...olumbia. Rick also volunteers his time helping to **conserve** ...urgeon living in the Fraser River.

Improving Quality of Life

Rick feels that it is important for people with physical disabilities to live their lives with greater independence. To help achieve this goal, he created the Quality of Life program. This program provides **grants** to people who have disabilities so they can make their homes more accessible with wheelchair ramps, and to help them pay for homecare, therapy, and exercise equipment. Rick's foundation also created an online tool called Planat, which allows people with disabilities to view and rate how accessible places are within their own communities and around the world.

A Proud Canadian

In 2012, Rick Hansen was appointed, or named, an Honorary Colonel of The Joint Personnel Support Unit (JPSU), which is a program that supports members of the Canadian Armed Forces who are unable to work due to illness or injury. As an Honorary Colonel, Rick is responsible for boosting the morale among members, and ensuring that the traditions of the Canadian Armed Forces are kept alive.

Rick motivated students to reach for their dreams at the Rick Hansen Secondary School in Mississauga, Ontario, in 2011.

hool Days

hen Rick wasn't wheeling during his Man in Motion World Tour, days were spent talking to the media, visiting hospitals, and ivering speeches at schools and community events. Today, Rick ntinues to visit schools to motivate dents to be all that they can be, spite their different abilities. In preciation of Rick's efforts and dication, schools are named after n throughout Canada.

> "
> *I believe that anything is possible, and that when there is a barrier, either physical or emotional, you can always find a way around it, or over it, or under it.*
>
> **—Rick Hansen,**
> **www.rickhansen.com**
> "

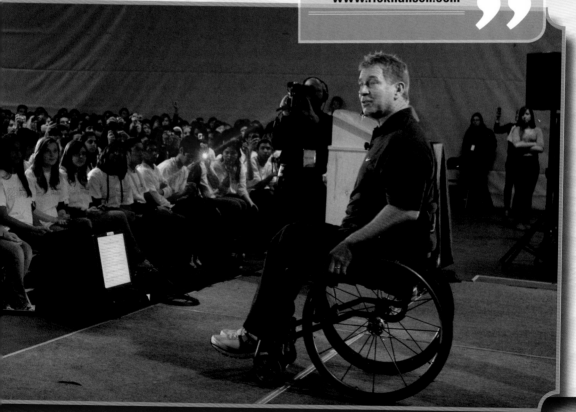

Writing Prompts

1. What personal characteristics do you believe are important to achieve your dreams? Which of these do you see in Rick Hansen?

2. What do you think Rick's greatest achievement is? Why?

3. In what ways has Rick's Man in Motion World Tour inspired others?

4. Do you feel that your own school and community are inclusive to people with disabilities? What are some ways to improve the accessibility at these places?

5. Has Rick Hansen's story inspired you to reach for your goals? How?

6. Why does Rick believe that the wheelchair will one day only be seen in a museum?

7. How has Rick changed people's attitudes toward disabilities?

Learning More

Books

k Hansen: Man in Motion. Rick Hansen and Jom Taylor. Douglas and McIntyre. 11.

k Hansen: A Life in Motion. Don Quinlan. Fitzhenry and Whiteside. 2013.

l On: Rick Hansen Wheels Around the World. Ainslie Manson. Greystone Books 1. 2013

k Hansen. Terry Barber. Grass Roots Press. 2008.

k Hansen: Canadian Hero. Pearson Canada. 2004.

Websites

vw.rickhansen.com

k Hansen's official website featuring information about The Man in Motion World ir as well as up-to-date information about his work today.

vw.rickhanseninstitute.org/

rn about the ways the Rick Hansen Institute is helping to improve the lives of ople living with disabilities.

vw.speakers.ca/speakers/rick-hansen/

it this website to watch videos of the Man in Motion World Tour, as well as erviews with Rick Hansen.

vw.sportshall.ca

id about Rick and other Canadian athletes at the official website of Canada's Sports l of Fame.

vw.thecanadianencyclopedia.ca/en/article/rick-hansen/

s interactive site is Canada's national encyclopedia, which provides information ut Canada and its people. Read an article on Rick Hansen here.

Glossary

conserve To prevent the wasteful or overuse of a resource

escort A group of armed guards that protect a person as they move from one place to another

exhibition sport A sport that is played at sporting events to promote it, or draw attention to it

grant Money given by an organization to support a particular cause

inclusive Including everything or everyone

morale The enthusiasm of an individual or a group of people

paraplegic Someone affected by paralysis of the legs and lower body

physiotherapist A person who uses physical methods, such as massage, to treat disease and injury

pilates Exercise that improves physical strength, posture, and flexibility

rehabilitation Treatment to restore a person's health through therapy and training

spinal cord The column of nerve tissue enclosed within the spine. The spinal cord forms the central nervous system and connects nearly all parts of the body to the brain

stigma Negative and unfair beliefs that a people have about something or someone

Index